love and love lost

love and love lost
poems and lyrics

by lulu gordon

abracadabrapress

Abracadabra Press
www.abracadabrapress.com

Lulu Gordon
www.lulugordon.com
lulu@lulugordon.com

ISBN # 978-0-615-31916-2

Cover photo by Mark Gurvis
Cover design by Lyn Bishop

abracadabrapress

acknowledgements

Special thanks to my dear brother and sister-in-law, Robert and Joyce, for their support and encouragement. Thanks also to my editor, Lisa Alpine, for her guidance and vision. And, much love to my very own posse of yaya sisters, Katie, Kat, Kim, Nene, Lisa, Paula and Elizabeth, for their friendship, wisdom and unflagging enthusiasm.

abracadabrapress

for canyon boy

contents

introduction

Love is worth the pain
We're broken hearted now
but we'll be back again
-Ray Charles

A friend of mine asked, "Do you think you can die of a broken heart?" I didn't know, though, it might be preferable if we could. How many times can our hearts be broken and keep on loving, and keep falling in love?   Medical science tells us that our skin, liver and spleen are the only organs that naturally regenerate themselves, but clearly, our hearts do it all the time. I can attest to that fact.

"Would I have been willing had I known the cost, a shattered heart and love lost?"

Emphatically yes. Over and over. I have been told that I am a hopeful romantic. It's true. I believe in love. I like to think that love's wear and tear leaves our hearts with a burnished patina. The loves of my life have given me so many lasting treasures; from Coltrane to baseball, hockey to karmic healing, first love to true love, love songs and a guitar. In fact, my lyrical journey began with that guitar...

love and love lost

guitar in hand

There he was
smiling
a steel-stringed guitar
in hand
a beautiful Martin
ready for love

A leap of faith
an act of courage
His face a mixture of excitement
and trepidation

Would I hear the music
as he did?
Did he see the music in me
waiting to happen?

I said yes to the gift
Not just the beautiful Martin,
but the faith
that my soul would
embrace the music

I was willing to take
the journey
wherever it led me

And what a lovely journey it has been

transition angel

Full of magic
Full of music
Full of love

Takes me to Paris
and paradise
and purgatory too

Is the journey almost ending
or has it just begun
Is our song almost over
or yet unsung

Sing me a lullaby
Wrap the words around
my aching soul
as I travel along this
transition road

the heart wants
what it wants

Throughout history
love's been a mystery
It will always be that way
Let's enjoy the ride another day

The heart wants what it wants
And it wants you
No rhyme or reason, just the truth
Nothin' you can do

Don't even try
It won't be denied
It's why we're here
so hold me close and dear

The heart wants what it wants
And it wants you
No rhyme or reason, just the truth
Nothin' I can do

It's not complicated
It can't be dissuaded
It was meant to be
Let's make this feeling last for eternity

The heart wants what it wants
And it wants you
No rhyme or reason, just the truth
Nothin' we can do

The heart wants what it wants
And it wants you

first love

green eyes
lit with mischief
and
his laugh
a reckless
explosion
of glee

teasing

body
strong
thick
graceful
pressed against me

igniting

skin
golden
smooth
smelling of sun
and sea

intoxicating ➤

voice
rich
melodic
singing with Cat Stevens
on the eight track

serenading

first love

discovering

 me

true blue goodbye

True Blue had hazel eyes
He was handsome
movie-star handsome
Thick dark hair, aquiline nose
A hockey player with perfect teeth
Tall, dark and handsome
Completely unaware of
his own wow

True blue in every way
"When a Man Loves a Woman"
true blue
Whatever the problem
loving me, was his solution
He was my hero

We found passion
I taught him about pleasure
he taught me about devotion

I walked away
the summer of our 4th year
No apparent reason
that I can recall
Broke his heart
and my own

I wish I could tell him
I'm sorry

Sorry I betrayed his
true blue ways

out of the blue goodbye

He was brilliant
He was compassionate
He slow-danced me to Coltrane
He understood my journey
saw through the mess
to the best of me
He was crazy about me

Out of the blue
I said goodbye
 "because"
just because

Later, I realized
because it was perfect
He is the one that got away

He is still brilliant
compassionate

crazy about me

There is some solace in that

diamond in the rough

He was just a man
a dear, wounded man
came without a plan
a sparkler
a soulful soul
unpolished by love
a diamond in the rough

We were drawn to each other
we could not resist
but our wounds
could not co-exist

We parted with pain
and regret
Much to remember
and much to forget
Waiting and waiting
for time to heal
as time
we know
will do

in time

memories of you

left side of the bed
strong tea in the morning
black coffee in the afternoon
long showers
soap from Spain
After Tan
hate the cold
love the sun
Mike Royko
Ernie Banks
Kirk Gibson's homerun
sausage on your pizza
sandwiches dry, hold the mayo
The Honeymooners
Crime Story
a penchant for mob movies
Luca Brasi swims with fishes
editor extraordinaire
- articles *everywhere*
funny faces, inciting laughter
- *every time*
jazz, jazz, jazz
your favorite things
your favorite places
your wounds
your gifts
your heart
your soul

endear and endure

bluesville

All dressed up
with nowhere to go
but Bluesville
Paying the price of indecision
with regrets that could kill

What's a girl like me
doing in a life like this
lost in the abyss of Bluesville

Old wounds haunt
like ghosts seeking solace
but there's no escaping the past

Wondering if
I could exchange my heart
for a newer model
with less wear and tear
and a GPS out of Bluesville

What's a girl like me
doing in a life like this
lost in the abyss of Bluesville

Wish I knew then
what I know now
How the good life flies by
with or without you

Before time runs out
I've got to find my way
find my way out of Bluesville

a gamblin' man

He was a gamblin' man
he meant no harm
Always got along on
good looks and charm

He bet our money
he bet our love
he bet his lucky stars above

But the money ran out
and the luck did too
his charm wasn't enough
to see us through

Never thought of tomorrow
just lived for today
In the end
he gambled my heart away

Too bad he didn't see
the writing on the wall
didn't notice the house of cards
was gonna fall   ➤

I tried to tell him
tried to show him the way
but he just couldn't hear
what I had to say

He says I broke his heart
when I left that day
but he broke mine first
when he gambled it away

I wish him well
Hope he finds love again
Hope he's learned
some things
you just can't mend

divestiture

Time to divest
Pull up stakes
Put a brake
on this heartbreak
Close the hope account
Withdraw my soul
Stop throwing good heart
after bad

The love funding
is done
'cause you're not
the one
You're overdrawn
credit is gone
This bad investment
calls for reassessment

Now I see
I need a new strategy
one that provides me
sweet love
and harmony

a reminder

I leave the photograph on my dresser
Me, at three
swinging on a swing
bright eyed
big smile
carefree

It's a "before" picture

Before the disappointments
Before the things that happened
and didn't happen
Before self-doubt
Before love
and love lost

I leave the photograph on my dresser
to remind me
of how it was
and how it can be again

moonlight in vermont

17 versions of *Moonlight in Vermont*
Stan Getz, Sonny Stitt, Charlie Byrd
Chet Baker, Willie Nelson, Joe Pass,
Tony, Ella and Frank,
to name a few

What would possess some one
to collect
17 versions of
Moonlight in Vermont

Truth is, they are like old friends
keeping me company
emotionally reliable
always deliver what they promise
that perfect balance
of melancholy and serenity
like a well-made
Manhattan or Martini
Each version sings a different song
each perfect in its own way

The perfect music to feel lonely by
The perfect music to love by
1 hour and 56 minutes of solace
for whatever ails me
How was my day?
Never mind
just
Moonlight in Vermont me

returned to single status

"Nothing more to be done
you are returned to single status
on the date in the order."
Her words caught me off guard
I gave her an uncomprehending look
"Pardon?"

"You are returned to single status
on that date." She said again

"You don't have to come back in.
We have streamlined the process
now it happens automatically."

Nothing
was
emotionally stream-lined
about separating our lives
every aspect of it
had
a
jagged edge

Nothing
had been automatic
every step
had been
arduous
angst-filled   ➤

You are "returned" to single status

I was pretty sure that wasn't an option
The check boxes are:
     Single
     Married
     Divorced
     Widowed

No "returned" option

Why doesn't "single" suffice?
 are they asking
 "damaged single?"
"sad single?"
"angry single?"
Or perhaps
"single but wiser?"

I am single
and I hope wiser

man enough
to be my man

True love's not for the faint of heart
you gotta have guts and faith from the start
We never know what the future holds
so make your move, let your heart be bold

Are you brave enough for love that's true
are you strong enough to see it through
are you smart enough to understand
are you man enough to be my man

Don't quit baby, when it gets too real
jump right in, don't be afraid to feel
if your heart gets broken, it will mend
it'll all be worth it in the end

Are you brave enough for love that's true
are you strong enough to see it through
are you smart enough to understand
are you man enough to be my man

No don't hold back, don't you resist
'cause honey darlin', this is it
surrender to it, stay here with me
true love's a gamble, but it'll set you free

Are you brave enough for love that's true
are you strong enough to see it through
are you smart enough to understand
are you man enough to be my man

waiting my life away

waiting my life away

waiting for the storm to pass
hoping for a calm that lasts
waiting for love that is true

waiting for you

waiting to breathe in and out
hoping to resolve the doubt
waiting for life to start anew

waiting for you

waiting for it to be my time
hoping to leave the past behind
waiting for grey skies to turn blue

waiting for you

waiting for that sunny day
hoping to find my way
waiting for my dreams to come true

waiting for you

sweet man

The timbre of his voice
deep
enthralling
calling to me

The easy touch
of his eager hands
wanting
waiting

Blue eyes
desiring
admiring
irresistible

Idiosyncratic walk
of an aging warrior
joints and muscles
having the last laugh

A big heart
buried deep
revealed
for brief
brilliant
moments
worth waiting for

Oh, Sweet Man

strummin' guitar
'neath the starry sky

He is shy with a song but his hands are strong
They find their way before too long
Strummin' guitar 'neath the starry sky

Hangin' around with my sweet guy
Strummin' guitar 'neath the starry sky
My big guy, the guitar and the starry sky

Oh it feels so right with the moon on bright
To be in his arms all through the night
Strummin' guitar 'neath the starry sky

Wish it could always be this way
Playin' guitar every night and day
Laughin', lovin' and singin' out loud
'Neath the starry sky

Singin' our songs brings such bliss
Heaven can't be better than this
Strummin' guitar 'neath the starry sky

Hangin' around with my sweet guy
Strummin' guitar 'neath the starry sky
My big guy, the guitar and the starry sky

My sweet guy, the guitar and the starry sky

desolation riff

The heart waits
with
syncopated
beats
of wanting

the body waits
moving
to a subliminal
rhythm
of longing

the mind waits
ignoring
the crescendo
of a familiar
desolation riff

she waits
every gesture
bearing the
weight
of desire

ranger romp

The telephone rings
my heart sings
It's Ranger Man on the line
he's got "a little window" of time
and it's all mine
How sublime

I'm on a tear
now, what to wear?
fix my hair
a little perfume too
can't hardly wait
to open the gate
and let ol' blue eyes through

Tee shirt and jeans
smile pristine
looks so fine
smells divine

I breathe him in
makes my head spin
I'm weak in the knees
looking to please
and I know he is too

We're on our way
no further delay

Oh, that Ranger Romp we do

magic

Magic's
what you are to me
Your magic's
 where I want to be

It lights my heart
It feeds my soul
It's got hold of me
and won't let go

It pulls me close
and closer still
Every magic moment
a breathless thrill

How lucky
to have felt its power
How treasured
each magic hour

So thanks
for the abracadabra days
And the gift
of your magic ways

For while you, my dear,
are now long gone
Your magic spell
lingers on

soulmates in song

We found each other
soulmates in song
It was our destiny
all along
Like two song birds
happy and free
me for you and
you for me

Wrapped in the music
we're just boy and girl
in a dreamy place
our own little world
free from worries
trouble and woe
a secret safe harbor
that only we know

Where the music flows
and the wine does too
Where our hearts ignite
and our love is true
Where *every* song
is our favorite song
Where our souls dance together
Where we belong

our songs

He gave me songs
First by others
then his own

They spoke the words
he could not
Although
he would deny this

Like waves on the shore
I never tire of hearing them

Like sand dollars on the beach
my heart collects them

If our lives were but a song

azure blue

Eyes azure blue
with cobalt shadows
of soul beneath

Inviting exploration of
the secrets
hidden
within his
red coral creviced heart

Buried treasure of love
awaiting discovery

lulu's diner

Honey, just for you
Lulu's Diner
is open 24/7
Yes, anytime
day or night
you can order up
some homemade heaven

The menu varies
from day to day
but you can always
have it your way
Darlin', you can get
anything you want
just like *Alice's Restaurant*

There's no need
to go down the block
or across the street
to that coffee shop
'cause what Lulu serves up
can't be beat
Why not rise and shine
to a breakfast treat? ➤

Five meals a day
or just one or two
Lulu is happy
to cater to you
Whenever you're hungry
whatever
you're hungry for
place your order with Lulu
and then order some more

Try the Daily Special
it's sure to please
Her secret sauce
will bring you to your knees
But you had better save room for that pie
guaranteed to satisfy

Whether you take your time
 or just in and out
The food's so good
it will make you shout
Yes Lulu's Diner, open 24/7
Step in, Sugar
for some Lulu heaven

one man woman blues

My Baby done told me
from the start
Said he would break my
lovin' heart
That's what he said
that's what he did
So it ain't news
I got the blues

I got a two woman man
and the one man woman blues

He said he was trouble
he would make a mess
I didn't believe him
I must confess
I was a fool
such a fool
A man of his word
He's got me singing the blues

I got a two woman man
and the one man woman blues   ➤

He makes my body tremble
When he plays lover man
He keeps me satisfied
Like no other can
I've got it bad
I've got the blues

'Cause I'm just one woman
And my man, he needs two

I said Sugar
I can never win
I'll be singing these blues
again and then again
I'm gonna lose
I'm gonna lose
So it ain't news
I got the blues

I got a two woman man
and the one man woman blues

too much
information blues

Just when I'm feelin' fine
forget you're not all mine
thinking life is sweet
and love is true

I get some incidental,
accidental
piece of news
and I'm lost in the
too much information
blues

I'm told ignorance is bliss
I can see the sense in this
so I do my best
to live in the present

Then I get some incidental,
accidental
piece of news
and I'm lost in the
too much information
blues ➤

Don't read the paper
avoid the TV too
I already know why
the world has got the blues
and just when I think
I've escaped the bad news

I get some incidental,
accidental
news of you
And I'm lost in the
too much information
blues

Heard the truth will set you free
hasn't worked that way for me
I'm still here in the land
of hopes and dreams

Then I get some incidental,
accidental
piece of news
and I'm lost in the
too much information blues

Yes, I'm lost in the
too much information
blues

perpetually star-crossed

Perpetually star-crossed
our love
is love lost
From the perfect first kiss
a tragedy
wrapped in bliss
But we couldn't resist

Twenty years too late
or a lifetime too early
doesn't really matter
it doesn't change
our story

You know it too
my dear
nowhere to go
from here
What would Romeo
and Juliet do?
Pick their poison
and be through
Seems a little dramatic
for me and you ➤

So we'll kill
our hearts and souls
instead
It's almost
like being dead
Except for the pain
the exquisite pain
Of knowing we will
never love again

Now walk away
walk away
don't look back
Ignore the heartache
the heartbreak
the panic attack

We will move through life
as if we're fine
and I suppose
our hearts
will heal with time
But our love will continue
on and on
forever
we'll hear
its quiet song

gracious goodbye

A gracious goodbye

So the memory of our magic
can fill us full
of joy
to last a lifetime

a life apart

So the sound of our music
can be called to mind
whenever needed

So our hearts can continue
their dance of love

in some parallel universe

memory riptide

They said their goodbyes
sweet and tender
and just like that
they walked away
back
to their very separate lives

But the memories come
without warning
of places, words, phrases
that belonged to them
songs, things said and unsaid
bodies wrapped around
a Paris state of mind

Memories held in the senses
of touch, smell, sound
pulling them back
into a sea of emotions
like a dangerous undertow

They fight the riptide
swimming hard
to the future
a future
safe
from memories

back in the fight

I can see now
that nothing's changed
Everything's going to stay the same
The things that broke my heart before
will break my heart again

My heart is like a weary boxer
in the corner of the ring
bruised and broken
from trying to win
Do I have enough heart
to get back in the fight?
Some form of smelling salts
that will revive and ignite?

The crowd is calling for a TKO
They can't bear to see
the fatal blow
I fought like a warrior
full of love's fire
but maybe they're right
it's time to retire   ➤

'Cause there's no fight
left in me
anymore
Can't even recall
what I was fighting for
A dream, a life
that could never exist?
Seemed so real
so right
It was hard to resist

Well, it's all gone now
no champions here
Nothing left to win
Nothing left to fear
Would I have been willing
had I known the cost?

A shattered heart and
love lost

how could you?

how could you walk away
from all we had
how could you turn our love
from good to sad

how could you take something
so full and sweet
and reduce it to something
so small and meek

how could you squeeze the life
out of larger than life

help me understand
I need to know
did it make it easier
for you to go?

was your broken heart reprieved
while a lethal dose of tepid
is what mine received

wouldn't it have been better
full strength until the end
wouldn't that have made it easier
for broken hearts to mend

magic slayer

magic slayer
nay sayer
kill joy too
hope dasher
dream trasher
no follow-through
wet blanket
a real drag and
no can do

well, screw you

reticent
reluctant
recalcitrant
ridiculous
glass half empty
and heart half ass

think I'll take a pass

hell cat

Wild cat
Hell Cat
hell to pay

Something you said
or didn't say
What can you do
to make her stay?

Your love is true
Can she see you,
your point of view?
Her heart is yours
of this you're sure
So what is the magic cure?

Arrest her with love
Restrain her with your songs
Jail her in your arms
where she belongs
Handcuff her with laughter

until

as sure as the fog rolls in
your Hell Cat
starts to purr again

paris, in love

Most folks have to fly
across the sea
And some folks have to fly
across the country
But Darlin', we're the lucky ones
'cause whenever we're together
we're in Paris
Paris, In Love

I'm not talkin' about
Paris, France
No I'm not talkin' about
Paris, Texas
I'm talkin' about
where love takes us
Paris, In Love

We don't need walks
along the river Seine
We don't need Mona Lisa,
or what's her name?
Forget the Eiffel Tower high above
'cause when we Waltz Across Texas
we're in Paris
Paris, In Love   ➤

I'm not talkin' about
Paris, France
No I'm not talkin' about
Paris, Texas
I'm talkin' about
where love takes us
Paris, In Love

I'm talkin' about Paris, In Love
(and it ain't no Peoria)
So take me to Paris, baby
It's where I wanna be
Take me to Paris, Darlin'
Just you and me
Take me to Paris
Paris, In Love

still on paris time

I'm still on Paris time
still in a Paris frame of mind
longing to be with you soon
under the spell of a Paris moon
longing to stroll the boulevards
beneath a blanket of Paris stars
Walking along the Seine each day
holding hands at Fleur café
people watching on the Champs Elysees

I'm still on Paris time
still in a Paris frame of mind
dreaming, my dear, of you
alone in that city made for two
Soon I will be back in your arms
back in Paris with all her charm
back in the City of Light
where hope springs eternal
and hearts take flight

until then

I'm still on Paris time
still in a Paris frame of mind
and there is no place
I would rather be
than with you, in Paris
toujours
mon Cheri

lingerie toujours

I believe in love
I also believe in lingerie
every day
- *toujours*
it inspires excellence
excitement
adventure
it is the *pièce de résistance*

it's an invitation to a party
a cause for celebration
an instigator
facilitator
communicator
and negotiator
extraordinaire

one should not underestimate
the persuasive power
of a great pair of
panties and bra   ➤

if a picture is worth
a thousand words
lingerie is worth
two thousand

night or day
home or away
at work or for play
consider lingerie

it is not a cure
not mind bending
life altering
heart breaking
soul awakening
or god sent

it is however

divine

love trance

First a kiss
then another
lips
wet, close
brush each other
bodies move
drawn together

Lost in time
out of the mind
in the senses
hands seek
and find

A touch here
a moan there
action
incites reaction
more craving
more satisfaction

Heat rising
breathing rushed
limbs tangled
faces flushed   ➤

Graphic words
of desire
increase the pleasure
and the fire

When at last
the ride is through
the trance clings
to me and you
It lingers awhile
and holds us still
Imprinting us
with love's thrill

whirlwind of wonderful

Takes my breath away
Heart pounding
Heart stopping
Tidal wave
I'm in a whirlwind of wonderful
And I can't stop now

Turns me upside down
And inside out
Turns me on and on
And wears me out
I'm in a whirlwind of wonderful
And I can't stop now

Sends me flying high
A thrill a minute
A crazy wild irresistible ride
I'm in a whirlwind of wonderful
And I can't slow down

Flies me to the moon
Stratospheric
Meteoric
Written in the stars
I'm in a whirlwind of wonderful
And I can't stop now

terms of endearment

Big Darlin / Little Darlin

Canyon Boy / Little Girl

Sweet Man / Sunshine

Warrior / Beauty

My Dear / My Dear

Honey / Little One

Lover Boy / Baby Doll

Sweetie / Tweetie

Ranger/ Girlie

Guitar Man / Song Bird

Blue Eyes / Butterfly

Boyfriend / Girlfriend

Each term of endearment
a little gem
a gift of love
an "I love you" in disguise
Sweeter words
were never spoken

canyon boy

Canyon boy so near to me
his loving eyes still can't see
Conversations lost in canyon walls
from the mountain top his breathless calls

Change comes hard, the path unmade
fearless warrior, yet so afraid
Moments of joy and moments of pain
each meeting spirits soar again

Guitar serenades into the night
song fest, love fest
it feels so right
Alone again in the dark of night

Falling behind, then side by side
ebb and flow of the passion tide
Moving fast, moving slow
can't say yes, oh, but can't say no

We find each other again and again
and push the future around the bend
Will this magic find a way
forever after or just fade away

Guitar serenades into the night
song fest, love fest
it feels so right
Alone again in the dark of night
Alone again in the dark of night

grown-up lullaby

Go to sleep my weary warrior
Let sweet dreams take you away
And when you wake unto the mornin'
You will find a brand new day

Rest your head upon the pillow
Soon your troubles will be gone
Slow the rhythm of your breathin'
Until the nighttime meets the dawn

Don't you fret about tomorrow
Rest here easy in my arms
Let go of all your worldly worries
I will keep you safe from harm

Surrender to that blissful slumber
Relax your handsome furrowed brow
Warm days and blue skies await you
So let the darkness have you now

goodbye

I wrote a goodbye letter
so I would get it right
when the time came
So many iterations
of the same sad truth
hoping that one revision
or another
would bear the epiphany
of a perfect solution
to our love conundrum

No epiphany arrived
No amount of revising
provided relief

When the letter
was perfectly perfect
and perfectly poetic
I put it aside
I did not have the will
or the desire to
to say those words

I had been in a rush
I thought a broken heart
was preferable
to a bitter heart
but the heart adapts
and the heartbreak
would keep
for a later date
a more convenient time ➤

I couldn't leave
when it was rough
the romantic in me
wanted it to end
on a sweet note
that could be
remembered
and
replayed

and
replayed

I couldn't leave
when it was sweet

because

it was too sweet
to leave

There would never be
a convenient time
to say goodbye
We made several
valiant attempts
to no avail
And that perfectly
perfect
goodbye letter
remains tucked in a file
somewhere   ➤

I have stopped worrying
about when
or how
to leave

I have stopped worrying
about when
or how
we'll say goodbye

Everything
that ever need be said
on the subject of
goodbye
has already been said
between us

except

goodbye

end of summer

It was the end of summer
and the end of love
not the summer of love
but a summer of
unspoken goodbyes
unanswered questions
unfinished dreams
love undone

the summer fog rolled in
and drifted out
hills turned pale blond
creeks stilled to a whisper
gardens bloomed
and went to seed
gravensteins arrived

It was the end of summer
the end of love

o v e r

Over
Completely finished
and oh so done
Overdone
Over the euphoria
and desire
Over him
being over me
Still, I play it over
and over
It's been overplayed
"Get over it"
wish it were that easy
Over, easy
It's over
over the waiting
over the worst of it
over him
out of love
over and out

never got over you

Well Darlin' it's been a while
a long lonesome while
since I've seen your smile
Such a long time since
you sang me a song
since we've danced together
it's been so long

Can't say I ever got over you
Can't say I ever wanted to

I know I should have done
should have found someone
who could take my heart
and change my mind
convince me to leave you behind
I should have moved on down
the line

But I couldn't forget about you
Can't say I ever wanted to   ➤

No I don't want someone new
'cause for me, there's only you
You made my heart yours
And I don't want a cure
true love always finds a way
you'll be mine one day

I know it won't be long
'cause love this right, can't be wrong
you'll walk back through my door
laughin' and lovin' me like before
'cause our love is true love
a once in a life time love

Can't say I ever got over you
Can't say I ever wanted to

No I'll never get over you

the middle of the bed

Lately I find myself
sleeping in the middle of the bed
Feather pillow soft underneath my
dream-filled head

Couldn't foresee that I would be
sleeping in the middle of the bed
I'm not complaining, it has its benefits
Room to move, room to breath
lights on or off as I see fit

But the sheets are ice cold and
there's no one breathing next to me
Turns out the middle of the bed can be
mighty lonely

It wasn't part of my plan
It wasn't part of my story
and for true love
I'd gladly surrender
my king-sized territory

Until then, I'll be
sleeping in the middle of the bed
Feather pillow soft underneath my
Dream-filled head

wishful thinkin'

Dancin' that dance
holdin' his hand
wonderin' could he be my man
Was my searchin' done
Maybe he could be the one

But it was just wishful thinkin'
that I could love him too
Just wishful thinkin'
that I could forget about you

His kisses were sweet
as he held me tight
He sure seemed like Mr. Right
Could he steal my heart away
Would he save the day

But it was just wishful thinkin'
that I could love him too
Just wishful thinkin'
that I could forget about you

He was kind and
generous to a fault
everything a girl could want
Asked me to go with him
I was plannin' to say yes

But it was just wishful thinkin'
that I could love him too
Just wishful thinkin'
that I could forget about you   ➤

'Cause Darlin' he can't make me laugh
the way you do
I don't feel that magic
like I do with you
tell me what I'm supposed to do

Guess I'll just keep lookin'
for love that's true
maybe someday I'll find someone
just like you
someone, just like you

That's just wishful thinkin'
Just so much wishful thinkin'

if only you knew

I had to leave you behind
Hopin' to find some peace of mind
but I've come to see
like a song, you're still with me

If only you knew
I'm here, lovin' you
If only you knew
my heart is with you

Wake every day the same way
dreamin' of your sweet kiss
feel your warm embrace
recall your handsome face

If only you knew
I'm here, lovin' you
If only you knew
my heart is with you

Do you still sing your song to me
each and every day
Do you remember
my lovin' ways
Would you come find me
Make me yours
Make me yours ➤

Wishin' my heart would mend
Longin' to hold you again
Wonderin' if you had the chance
would I be your last romance

If only you knew
I'm here, lovin' you
If only you knew
my heart is with you

My heart is still with you

estimated time of arrival

When do we arrive in our own lives

Feels like my life hasn't started
yet it is more than half over
I'm on the fringe
outside looking in

When will observing turn to living
What am I waiting for
as present turns to future

Time passes by as
I seek a safe landing
With no place in sight
I keep circling my own life

ETA

has been delayed

metamorphosis

Uniquely
Stupid
Undesirable
Loser Girl

Has
to
get
better, right?

Can't
feel
this
way
forever, right?

Uniquely
Stupendous
Irresistible
Lover Girl

Hmm,
much better

heart patina

I've had my share
of love's wear and tear
weathered the losses
some
better than others

When my heart
is quiet again
on the mend
I find treasures
left behind
for the taking

And so
this heart of mine
patinas with time
burnished
and better for the wear
it beats on
to a silent love song
ready
willing
and waiting

just around the corner

Don't know when
don't care how
but I know
he's just around
the corner now

Don't know the place
But I'll know his face
His voice will be
my sweet song
his arms, where
my soul belongs

Don't know when
don't care how
but I know
he's just around
the corner now

He'll see my face
and know it's me
I'll sing to him
and set him free
wherever I am
he will be   ➤

We won't need cupid's arrow
to figure it out
It will be clear as day
no room for doubt
Heaven sent
and right as rain
like comin' home again

Don't know when
don't care how
but I know
he's just around
the corner now

Just right around
the corner

come home to me darlin'

Come my dear
Come home to me

Come sing me a song
a sweet melody

About the trees and starlight
and mountains to climb
about gardens that grow
and your favorite pastimes

Make the ordinary
extraordinary
as only you do

Come home to me Darlin'
I'm waiting for you

hopeful romantic

I believe in love
the power of love
the magic
felt across a crowded room
the poetry of that
perfect
first kiss

I believe in hearts on fire
and the heat of love's desire
in making plans
and holding hands
in leisurely walks
and long talks
in stolen glances
and second chances

I believe in missing
and longing
and belonging
in butterflies
and weak in the knees
in the promise of a starry night
and slow dancing by pale moonlight ➤

I believe in wistful goodbyes
and blissful hellos
in love letters
and love songs
in saying "I love you"
in candlelight
and making love all night

I believe in new love
out of the blue love
true love
and
love you always dreamed of
in love that never ends

I believe that love lost
can be found again

about the author

Lulu Gordon has evolved from married to single, urbanite to Marinite, lawyer to poet. She is younger now. And wiser. A happier version of herself. Briefcase discarded. She now comes armed with pigtails, poetry and a guitar, sharing her adventures of love and love lost.

abracadabrapress